FORGOTTEN

FORGOTTEN

A JOURNEY INTO FRIENDSHIP

Delphine Levesque

authorHOUSE®

AuthorHouse™
1663 Liberty Drive
Bloomington, IN 47403
www.authorhouse.com
Phone: 1-800-839-8640

Published by AuthorHouse   03/22/2013

ISBN: 978-1-4817-1938-4 (sc)
ISBN: 978-1-4817-1937-7 (e)

IN GRATITUDE TO
Father Richard DiGiulio

Those we Love remain with us
For Love itself lives on
And Cherished Memories never fade
Because a Loved One is gone . . .
Those we Love
Can never be more than a thought apart
For as long as there is a Memory
They'll live on in the Heart.

Author Unknown

Our dead are among the invisible,
not among the absent.

Pope John XXIII

CONTENTS

ABOUT THE TITLE

It is a good and comforting feeling to be remembered at anytime and in any way. That unexpected card in the mail that says someone is thinking of you, or the birthday cards that begin to accumulate just before your special day remind you that you are loved.

But to be forgotten hurts. That thought came to me once years ago when I happened to pass a very neglected cemetery. I thought about what it must have been like when each one of those graves was fresh and the mourners remembered the departed one for some years thereafter. Then as time passed, they were forgotten. When I got home, the poem *Forgotten* came to me and I wrote it out just as you see it here. I added it to my portfolio. It wasn't until 2008 that it had significance.

FORGOTTEN

How many times in passing
I turn my head to gaze
Upon the sea of headstones
That stand amidst the maze
Of row on row of sorrow
Where tears have greened the grass
And lives of long-lost loved ones
Are buried in the mass.

I smile to see the flowers
By that attended plot
But wonder in deep sadness
Of those that some forgot
As time dissolves the memory
And others take their place
My heart sends out a prayer for them
May God their souls embrace.

FOREWORD

Delphine was born in South Bend, Indiana in 1939. She is the child of Sylvester and Lillian Szczechowski. Her primary education was in South Bend at St. Adalbert's Catholic School taught by the Felician Sisters.

She was raised from a devout Catholic family. She was formed in not only the teachings of the Church but also brought up in a prayerful atmosphere. Being a faithful and devoted follower of the Lord Jesus all her early life, led her to be enrolled in the Felician Sisters Convent in Livonia, Michigan in 1957. This was until 1970. Her life as a nun during those years only made her a more devoted disciple of the Lord Jesus.

In 1971 she married Robert Levesque. They have two children, David and Jennifer who are doing well. Robert and Delphine live in the Lockport, NY area. They are devoted members of St. Mary's Catholic Church in Swormville, NY.

As a result of Delphine's devotedness and prayerfulness, the Lord God has chosen her to be one of His instruments to pray especially for the deceased—those who are in purgatory. Actually, we are all called to pray for our brothers and sisters who have died. However, in a particular way Delphine has helped to point out the responsibility we all have in regard to this act of charity.

In this wonderful book entitled *Forgotten, A Journey Into Friendship*, there are numerous incidents indicating the desire for prayers of intercession with regard to the departed souls. This book would be a follow up from a book entitled *Get Us Out of Here!* by Nicky Eltz which tells the experiences of Maria Simma who was visited by the departed souls.

The Sacred Traditions of the Roman Catholic Church have always taught us to pray for one another. What better way to live this teaching than by praying for those who have died? It is also stated in the record book of Maccabees that it is good and proper to pray for those who have gone before us in the hope of the Resurrection.

Delphine's book gives witness to the importance of praying for our beloved dead. We know that even though our sins are forgiven, we need to be fully purified of the effects of sin. We need to go through a period of purification in this world or in the next. Our prayers on earth help those in this state of purgation.

Does not Jesus tell us to love one another as He has loved you? What better way in showing love to our brothers and sisters than by praying for them? We do this for each other on earth; we should do this for others in purgatory.

I thank Delphine for the writing of this book, which testifies to the importance of praying for our beloved dead. This is a most charitable work and I personally testify that much devoted work and love has gone into it. Hopefully, the effect of this book leads us to understanding that we are all brothers and sisters in Christ Jesus. We always need to pray for one another.

Father Richard DiGiulio

It is therefore a holy and wholesome
thought to pray for the dead,
that they may be loosed
from sins.

—2 Machabees 12:26

IN APPRECIATION

To my dear friend and mentor
Helene Lee
For help with editing

Special thanks to
Beth Fifield-Crane
For the blessing of her artistic talent

Honor her for all that her hands have done:
and let her works bring her praise . . .

Proverbs 31:31

PREFACE

I believe with all my heart that I must tell my story. From the moment that it all began on All Souls Day in November of 2008, I knew that God must have a purpose for permitting the Souls in Purgatory to visit me. After telling my husband and then a few trusted friends, I sought spiritual guidance from a priest, but was disappointed when he told me that the process of discerning the authenticity of my encounters was more than he would have time for. One priest friend graciously accepted Mass stipends and offered the Masses I had requested for these Souls. Another who via email invited me to consult him never responded when I communicated my questions.

Fortunately for me, I had the blessing of meeting Msgr. Richard Nugent who resided at St. Bernadette's Parish in Orchard Park, NY. He was the spiritual director of a prayer group from my parish in Williamsville,

NY. I met him at a gathering where I approached him, introduced myself, and asked if he had the time to guide me with something I had been experiencing. He kindly agreed for me to mail him copies of journal entries that I had been copiously keeping since November 2008. I put them in the mail without delay. It was a blessed day for me when Father Nugent sent this email on August 27, 2009.

Greetings Delphine! I read, with pleasure, your letters and your journal on the visits from the Holy Souls. The Lord has given you a special blessing and apostolate in assisting the Holy Souls in purgatory. You are blessed with a husband who affirms these manifestations of confined souls and assists you. He will be blessed by the prayers of the suffering souls. You are wise to keep a journal of the visits. Perhaps, someone would print your journal on a computer for future study and observation. In the meantime, I recommend that you continue doing what you have been doing and depend on the Holy Spirit and the Mercy of God. You are welcome to e-mail me, if you wish for any questions or problems. In Christ and Mary, Father Nugent. PS. Maybe we will meet again with Dawn and the Ladies of the Lord.

Knowing that a priest believed me filled my soul with peace and encouragement. Sadly, Father Nugent passed away two months later. I did meet with him again and with Dawn, when the two of us visited him in the ICU at Sisters Hospital where we prayed the Chaplet of the Divine Mercy at his bedside. He died the next day.

If you believe in Purgatory and have a devotion to Souls there, I know that what I reveal in these pages will most certainly inspire you to sacrifice and to pray more fervently for their release. They are depending on you. For the curious and the dubious, may God pour merciful love towards those Souls into your heart and into the hearts of every living Christian.

CHAPTER ONE

WHAT IS PURGATORY?

The dictionary defines *purgatory* as "a state or place in which, in Roman Catholicism and other Christian doctrine, those who have died in the grace of God expiate their sins by suffering." A key word in this definition is *expiate*. By definition, this word means, "To make amends or reparation for wrong-doing or guilt; atone for." In order to understand the dire need of Souls in Purgatory, an understanding of this belief is primary. Christians believe that we are saved from Eternal Damnation by the Blood of Christ shed for us on the Cross. That is known as *redemption* for our sins, the very reason why God Almighty sent His Only Begotten Son to Earth. In the Catechism of the Catholic Church it is stated as follows:

All who die in God's grace and friendship, but still imperfectly purified, are indeed assured of their eternal salvation; but after death they undergo purification, so as to achieve the holiness necessary to enter the joy of

1

Heaven. (1030)* The Church gives the name "purgatory" to this final purification of the elect, which is entirely different from the punishment of the damned. The Church formulated her doctrine of faith on Purgatory at the Councils of Florence and Trent. The tradition of the Church, by reference to certain texts of Scripture, speaks of a cleansing fire. (1031*)

It helps to understand this teaching by realizing that when, for example, you are issued a speeding ticket, you are surely sorry for this and are forgiven by society for the danger you caused as a driver. However, paying for that ticket is *atoning* for the action. The same goes for criminals who are given a sentence of time in jail. They have to "make up" to society for the transgression. As Catholics we are encouraged to remember the Souls in Purgatory by praying for their release because they are suffering there to make amends for their sins.

From the beginning The Church has honored the memory of the dead and offered prayers in suffrage for them, above all the Eucharistic sacrifice, so that, thus purified, they may attain the beatific vision of God. The Church also commends almsgiving, indulgences, and works of penance undertaken on behalf of the dead. (1032)*

In 1926 a book was published entitled "Purgatory Explained by the Lives and Legends of the Saints" written by Father F.X. Schouppe, S.J. It is filled with captivating stories of saints who experienced events that

*   Catechism of the Catholic Church

confirm the need for atonement for our sins in this life or in the hereafter in purgatory. We can assist the Souls in Purgatory by our prayers and sacrifices. What is little known is that the Souls themselves can help us here on earth or even intercede for our release from Purgatory once they are in Heaven.

CHAPTER TWO

SEEDS OF DEVOTION

Childhood influences can last a lifetime. I was raised in a Catholic home where certain practices were held as sacred. Saying our night prayers was very important, for example. I remember my dad turning down the radio to listen to me as I knelt by a chair in the dining room. On the wall there hung a picture of a guardian angel protecting two small children as they crossed a rickety old bridge. Church on Sunday at St. Adalbert's was a strict observance as was eating fish on Fridays.

My sisters and I went to the parish parochial school where Felician nuns taught us. I remember being very pious and impressionable as a child. Our teachers instilled into our young hearts a love for Our Blessed Mother and for all of the saints. I recall seeing a movie about St. Therese the Little Flower that was shown on the parish hall during Lent one year. From that time on, she was my favorite.

It was the custom during those days to honor the death anniversary of a deceased member of the parish by having a faux catafalque in the center aisle at the front of the church for a Mass of Remembrance. I can still see the altar boys setting this up and carefully placing the six tall black candleholders with the orange candles, three on each side of the casket after draping the black pall over the form. After Mass, the priest would come out dressed in a black cape. He prayed in Latin over this scene, and then blessed the casket with Holy Water. The smell of the incense from the censer swung by him added to the somberness of this ritual.

From the first grade on, the nuns inspired us to be pious children. We would pray for the Souls in Purgatory. "Eternal rest grant onto them, O Lord. And let perpetual light shine upon them. May the souls of the Faithful Departed through the mercy of God rest in peace. Amen!" We chanted with our small hands folded and pointed up to Heaven. I could not quite understand "purgatory", but a picture that I saw once of people in flames reaching up to Our Lady seared itself into my heart. All I could understand was that these people needed help to get to Heaven, and my prayers for them could make a difference. Holy cards and medals were things we got for being good children. I was so very proud of my collection.

My paternal grandparents lived upstairs from us. I remember that my Grandma Rose was a very religious woman. I always felt safe with her whenever a thunderstorm came along. She would come downstairs with her Holy Water bottle and bless all of the rooms and us kids as well. She wanted us to believe that God, Our Lady and the angels looked after us. She also taught us about remembering to pray for the Souls in Purgatory and how they would intercede to God for you if you asked them.

When I was older, she told me a story about an experience she had with them that changed my life forever. It seems that my grandfather was out of work once. Grandma Rose knew how powerful the prayers of the Souls were especially if you made a deal with them. She promised to have a Mass offered for their release from Purgatory if my grandfather found work.

Before long, he got a good job, but she forgot about her promise to the Souls. As she told me, she was awakened one night feeling a presence at the foot of her bed. Opening her eyes, she saw a light there and heard these works, "Remember that you promised us!" Immediately she realized that she had neglected to keep her end of the deal. The next morning she hastened to the parish rectory and arranged for a Mass for them.

This made a very big impression on me. Foremost, the visitation of Souls to my grandmother taught me that this was a serious thing. I understood that since they cannot pray for their own release, they must rely on us to obtain that grace from God.

In those days, there were no funeral parlors for wakes. The deceased person was viewed in the living room of the family home. My friends and I made it our business now and then to watch out for houses marked with a black bow and swag of fresh flowers on the front door. This indicated a place of mourning and visitation for guests to pay their respects. It was easy for me to boldly march up the front steps, enter the house and walk up to the casket, kneel down on the velvet-covered kneeler and say a prayer. I felt that it was something I must do.

During my thirty-year career in Catholic schools, teaching my students a love for the Souls in Purgatory was a priority. I wanted them to understand that when people "died", they really were just passing into another life. Having to spend time in Purgatory was God's plan for them to be purified. With all of the media emphasizing the fear factor when it comes to ghosts, I felt that the truth needed to be told. Whenever deceased persons make their presence known, they simply want our attention so that we will pray for them.

CHAPTER THREE

DAD

We were a very traditional Catholic family with Dad holding the place of supreme authority in our home. He was a strict but loving father who did not like the idea of having to spank his kids. He was very softhearted when it came to children in general, especially towards kids who were hard off. Whenever we were traveling from school and he saw children walking in inclement weather, he'd pull the car over to the curb and offer them a ride. In our neighborhood, this was an acceptable thing to do.

Daily family dinner was always at 5:30, and if you were even five minutes late, you were in trouble. Dad enjoyed Mom's cooking and always wanted us to appreciate that by being on time. He enjoyed food, so Mom made every meal hearty. I especially liked Fridays during the summer when we had the fresh fish that he caught the day before in a local lake. Served with the delicious tomatoes from his backyard garden, it was a treat!

I adored my father and always wanted to please him in everything I did. When the Lord called me away from home in 1957 to enter religious life, I know that it broke his heart. It was one of the biggest sufferings in my life to be separated from my family. After thirteen years and the repercussions of Vatican II, I left my order and soon married my husband. Dad was so happy for me!

As it turned out, we lived far away from my hometown, so once again I suffered that absence of being away from my family and all of its memorable events. That changed in June of 1978 when my husband took a job in Michigan, an hour away from my hometown. I was thrilled!

Sadly, my Uncle Andy was dying of cancer. Dad and he were like brothers and so this was very stressful for my father. I can remember the day like it was yesterday. The phone rang and it was my sister Louise calling with bad news. "Dad is dead," she said. "He suffered a massive heart attack." My body felt like stone. Here I expected to learn that Uncle Andy had passed away. All I remember is screaming and screaming. "NO! NO! NO!" Strangely, I had premonitions of this a couple of times before it happened. It was like God was preparing me for this dreadful moment.

I was filled with anger towards God, as I felt so cheated. Here after all of those many years of being away from my family, I was closer and now lost my father. I couldn't pray and I refused to go to church.

On the day of my Dad's funeral, my Uncle Andy died. Our family felt that Dad had asked God the Father to please relieve our uncle of his terrible suffering. Dad always had a way of convincing people of anything he felt strongly about. No exceptions!

A week later, I experienced my very first encounter with a departed soul. I was up on a ladder painting the front door of our new home. Now as a child, I loved to watch Dad painting around our house. I used to beg him to let me help. He'd just smile and say, "You just watch how I do it and learn. Some day you will have your very own house and you will get to paint all you want."

As I stretched to reach a high spot, I suddenly felt my Dad's presence, right there, behind me! It was if he was protecting me from falling backwards off that ladder.

"Why did you have to die?" I cried out loud as hot tears began to resurrect themselves from deep within my soul. "I just got here!" Had I turned around to look, I was certain I would have seen him.

"You are where God wants you to be right now," he said inside my soul. I felt a great sense of love and peace like never before. I think that I stood there on those ladder rungs for a long time, engulfed in the power of the moment.

For days afterwards, I dreamt about him. We would all be together in the old house enjoying some kind of family gathering and he'd suddenly come in the kitchen door. He'd stick around for a little, and then tell us that he had to get back. We were all content with that, believing that he was living with God in Eternity.

All that I believed about the Souls in Purgatory was not enough for me in my grief. I researched all available resources regarding the after life. I needed to know that the Catholic Church was not the only authority on this matter. To my surprise, I learned that many secular writers of the paranormal confirmed that the departed do need us to pray for them.

In time, my grief subsided and I was comforted by the fact that a physical body did not limit Dad to time and space. I believed that a loving and merciful God does allow our departed loved ones to be present to us on occasions. I made it a point to ask Dad for favors now and then, if only that he would look after me much like my angel does. As always in my life, I could count on him.

CHAPTER FOUR

FRANKIE

It was many years since that encounter with my Dad's spirit. The next event was when we were living in Lockport, NY and I was teaching second grade at St. Patrick's School. My classroom was a fun learning environment and the kids all got the word out to the lower grades about having me for their teacher.

I remember that it was the last day of school in June when a sandy-haired little boy approached me at the door during dismissal and announced, "Mrs. Levesque, I hope that I can be in your classroom next year!" I didn't know his name, but later learned that it was "Frankie." I replied, "Well, I hope so too!"

In the fall when we received our class roster, I noticed that a "Frankie" was on my list. In checking around, I realized that this was the same tyke that made that wish. Great! I was looking forward to this as I prepared the nametags for each student's desk. Nothing warms the heart of a teacher more than having enthusiastic children in the classroom.

Sadly a terrible tragedy occurred shortly before the first day of school that snuffed out the young life of this boy and his dad as well. The two of them were driving down Lockport Road to attend a wrestling match in Niagara Falls, NY when a truck ran a stop sign and smashed into their car. Both father and son were killed on impact. When I heard the news I was devastated! I needed to help Frankie's classmates cope with this loss. I decided to move his little desk next to mine and to keep it there all year in his memory.

The children talked about their friend a lot that first week of school. I remember the wake. There was a large closed ebony casket for the father, with a closed smaller white one next to it. It broke your heart to see the mother and grandmother, one who lost a husband and a son, the other, a son and grandson.

About a week after the funeral, I was in my classroom checking papers after school. Suddenly, I felt a presence, very much like I did when up on that stepladder years before after Dad had died. Tears filled my eyes as I said out loud, "Oh, Frankie! I am so sorry what happened to you and your father. I miss having you in my classroom this year." I covered my face and sobbed. Afterwards, I was filled with a strange sense of peace. I guess God sent this little messenger to me from Heaven. It is a memory that has stayed in my heart.

In honor of this father and son, the family planted a beautiful little tree on the grounds of the school with a plaque bearing their names and the date of their deaths. Whenever I drive by there today and see how large that tree has grown, I am reminded of that special day in September long ago when a little boy's spirit stood next to his desk and mine as if to comfort me. Such tragedies are a test of our faith and trust in God. We have only to envision the beauty and joy of Heaven to realize that a loving God sustains us during the trials and sufferings inflicted upon us in an imperfect world.

CHAPTER FIVE

HAUNTED HOUSES

The first time that my husband and I experienced anything paranormal in a house was in Rockport, Maine. We had our home built in the woods near a field that had a low stone border on one side. It looked so primitive, as if many years ago the stones were erected to keep small animals corralled.

After we moved in, I had the idea to have our house blessed by our parish priest. I kept putting it off because we were so busy. Soon we began to notice that doors we had shut would be opened, and vice versa. It was just about doors, nothing more. Sometimes we heard cupboards in the kitchen opening and closing. Soon we figured out that a spirit was haunting our house.

One day the contracting plumber came over to take care of a minor problem. I remarked to him about the strange door thing. He laughed and said, "I'm not surprised. This lot was part of old Indian burial grounds." Chills went up my spine. That explained that unusual stone fence. When I told this to my husband, he asked that I get the pastor over here to bless our home. Within a week, our home was prayed over and blessed.

With that done, we were content until doors started opening and shutting again. This time, I had a Mass offered for whatever Indian soul might be trying to get our attention. The strange phenomena ceased. I realized that the most powerful prayer for the departed is the Holy Sacrifice of the Mass.

Four moves later, we found ourselves living in a house snuggled in the woods in Birmingham, Alabama, where Bob was to start a new job. It was an interesting experience from the start. As in the past, I always prayed for God to guide us to wherever He wanted us to live. We had a great realtor who found a place she thought was most suitable for us, complete with a backyard pool. As we walked the rooms, I gasped when I saw a picture hanging on the wall in a hallway that was the exact same picture, frame and matting, of one that our daughter presented to my husband as a gift for his new office! She told us that while shopping at a mall a month earlier, she happened to be drawn into an art store for no apparent reason. When she spotted the picture of this lighthouse, she was compelled to get it for her dad. Bob being from Maine, of course, loves that kind of thing. Needless, to say, I knew that this particular house was exactly where God wanted us to live.

One night I awoke for no reason to the sound of a CLINK coming from the living room. I got up and went in there to determine the source. I turned on the light and realized that the sound was from a teacup being picked up and placed down on a shelf in my hutch. Well, I thought, someone is trying to get my attention.

The next morning when I shared this with my husband, he said, "You know, dear, there must be a tiny light above your head visible only to those spooks that know exactly where to come for prayers." So pray, I did.

Then one day my eyeglasses disappeared. I am a creature of habit and I always place them next to the Kleenex box on our vanity in the bathroom before I go to bed. That morning I had to search for them. When I pulled out the vanity stool to finally sit down to do my makeup, there they were, smack dab in the middle of the seat! Of course, some spirit put them there. Who else? A few days, later, I was sleeping with my back to my husband and was suddenly awakened by a push to my shoulder. Thinking it was Bob, I whispered, "What!" Well, since I heard him snoring softly, I knew that it was not he who had given me that shove. That was the first time that I was actually touched by a spirit. This sent a chill through my body, and I nestled closer to my hubby for the rest of the night.

This was getting serious, so I decided to do what we Catholics are advised whenever we feel that the departed are trying to get our attention: arrange for that Holy Mass to be offered for them. So the next day, I went to the parish rectory and did just that. Strangely, however, this did not put a stop to things.

Soon afterwards, our attention was solicited once again. We had just turned off the bedroom light to settle in for the night, when my husband and I heard a loud CLINK coming from the dresser. Obviously one of my perfume bottles had been lifted up and then loudly placed back on the glass tray.

"I thought you had a Mass offered," whispered my annoyed husband. "I most certainly did!" I angrily retorted. Well, I marched over to the rectory the next morning to see Father Mike. He advised that I check with the secretary to see if, indeed, she had placed the Mass on the schedule. Come to find out she had not. In our parish there seemed to be a backlog of Mass requests, and our Mass was not at the front of the list. At Father Mike's order, that Mass was put on the following week's schedule. I breathed a sigh of relief. Our guest was about to leave.

Soon afterwards, I had the occasion to speak with the original owners of our property when some of their mail came to the house by mistake. We chatted on the phone and in the process she made the remark that the folks we bought the house from had complained to her that the house was haunted.

"Oh, yes, indeed it was," I told her. I proceeded to tell her all of the ghostly encounters we had experienced and how we helped that poor soul with a holy Mass. She told me that the builder they contracted to construct their home went bankrupt. Shortly after this, the young man committed suicide. If this was his spirit pleading for my prayers, I am confident that he is resting in peace.

But this was not the end of our visitors from the other side.

CHAPTER SIX

STEPHANIE

The people from whom we bought the house had teenaged children. From what the neighbors told us, the parents frequently were gone to their lake house on weekends leaving their kids to host wild parties. In fact, this house got a reputation for dealing drugs. I learned that the neighbors were all anxious as to who the new owners were after we moved in wondering if we were drug dealers. Needless to say, when they met Bob and me, they were relieved.

One early morning in October, as I was backing the car out of the garage to leave for work, I noticed three men walking up our steep driveway. I found it odd that they did not come up in a vehicle. I rolled down my window and asked what they wanted. One of the men was carrying a woman's leopard skin handbag.

"Is this the Walker residence?" he asked. (Not the real surname.)

"No, they were the former owners from whom we bought the house."

"Do you know their new address? We need to get in touch with them."

"It's in the house. I'll get it for you." I hurried inside, copied the information down and returned full of anxiety over this strange encounter. As I handed them the slip of paper, they thanked me and then turned to go back down the driveway. I noticed the word "coroner" in white letters across the back of one man's black jacket.

That evening, I shared the entire conversation with my husband. We concluded that the purse must have belonged to the family's daughter, and that she had not changed the address on her driver's license after the family moved. We decided to watch the local newspaper everyday to see what might be reported.

Sure enough, in about a week there was an obituary listing the unexpected death of Stephanie, the oldest child of the Walkers. We heard from a neighbor that she had died of a drug overdose.

I knew that our guest room had been her bedroom. She had loved sunflowers and we had changed that to a roses theme. One night I had to sleep there because Bob's snoring was keeping me awake. Sometime during the night I awoke suddenly and looked over to the door that

I kept shut. It was open and a bright light was shining in the doorway. I got cold all over and felt very frightened. "Is that you, Stephanie child?" I whispered as I shut my eyes and pulled the quilt closer to my chin. This was another first for me. "If you are in distress and need my prayers, I promise that I will help you." Since my eyes were closed now, I had no idea what happened to the light or to the door until I woke up the next morning. The door was shut.

At breakfast, I asked my husband if sometime during the night he had gotten up, put the light on in the hallway and then came and opened my door. "Why on earth would I ever do that?" he asked. "Well, I just thought that you might have needed me for something." Of course, when I shared my encounter with a ghost, he smartly said, "Well, I guess it's off to the rectory for you." Well, indeed, I did just that. This time, the secretary wasted no time in putting the Mass intention on the roster. To this day, I remember Stephanie in my daily prayers for the Souls in Purgatory.

CHAPTER SEVEN

WITH LOVE FROM ROME

In 2003 my son and his wife went to Rome for their honeymoon. It was a wonderful experience for them. They especially enjoyed all the sights and sounds of the Vatican.

They both love to shop, so they made it a point to take advantage of the numerous little stores that lined the streets in the area. They wandered into a particular place that was filled with antiques, some of which were religious in nature. As David poked about, a very old and brittle picture caught his eye. For some reason he was inspired to purchase it for me. The clerk carefully packaged it between two pieces of cardboard and inserted it into a brown envelope.

We came to visit from Alabama after their return to hear about the honeymoon adventures. Deenna gave me a beautiful linen tablecloth and napkins for my teacart that they had picked up in Florence. David then said, "Mom, I don't know why but I thought that you would like this picture." I gasped when I opened the envelope and saw it! I felt that it was a special gift of love with a message for me. Here was Our Lady of Mount Carmel holding Baby Jesus Who Himself held scapulars in His Hands. Below was what I knew were the flames of Purgatory with the Souls confined there reaching up in supplication to Jesus and Mary. I had seen similar pictures of Our Lady interceding for the release of souls on other works of art. But this one was special because my son had thought of me in a distant country and carried home a message for me that would not take on a life of its own until November of 2008.

I remember asking Father DiGiulio about what role Our Lady plays in this grace that I have received. He said that it is our Holy Mother Mary Herself who chooses the souls who come to contact me. His affirmation reinforced the belief that Mary Herself guided my son into that shop in Rome and to that very special picture.

CHAPTER EIGHT

OUR LADY

After living in Birmingham, Alabama for seven and a half years, we decided to move back to Western New York to enjoy our first grandchild. God once again led us to this unexpected and life-changing decision. In our search for property to build on, I prayed for Divine Guidance, as it has always been important to me to be where God wanted us. We searched different areas, but kept coming back to the lot where we now live. Bob teased me, of course, and wanted to be certain that I prayed to the Souls in Purgatory for assistance.

On August 15, 2006, the Feast of the Assumption of Our Lady into Heaven, we moved our household into Vintage Court in Lockport, New York. I had a beautiful picture of the Sacred Heart of Jesus that used to hang in the kitchen of our house in Alabama. I had it in the car with us with the intention of giving it a first place of honor in our new home. That morning, we got to the house before the moving van. I walked inside holding the Sacred Heart picture, went straight to the fireplace mantle in the living room, and put it up in the center. "Lord Jesus, You have the honor of being the King of our new home, "I prayed. "Thank You for blessing this house with all the graces we need to please You. Amen."

After thirty-five years of marriage and this being our eighth move, we were finally settled near our children and grandchild. God saw in His wisdom that we would be needed as grandparents of this little boy, his little sister to come and Jenn and Frank's children as well. In time I began to realize what a grace this location was. The neighborhood is very quiet and the field and pond next to our backyard provide a prayerful setting.

One of the things Bob insisted on having was a four-season porch. This is where I go for my daily devotions and meditations. It reminds me of the "boat" that Jesus told His apostles to "always have ready", (Mark 3:9), the place where I can go when I need to shut out the noise and distractions of my busy world.

I always wanted to have an outside statue of Our Lady, so I had the landscaper design a grotto for Her. It was a joyful time for me when we unpacked the statue and placed it in the center of a circular stone-banked flowerbed. I felt happy knowing that I had honored Mary with this spot in my flower garden.

In parochial school, devotion to Our Lady was seriously instilled in the children. I was a member of the Sodality of Our Lady. During the induction ceremony, we were invested with a large Miraculous Medal attached to a wide pale blue ribbon. I still have this. I remember the beautiful May procession where Mary was crowned with flowers. I can still hear the traditional Marian hymns that I knew by heart. "Ave Maria" was my favorite.

During our first years in Alabama, I had the opportunity to make pilgrimages to the Field of the Caritas Community in Sterrett, AL that promotes and supports the apparitions of Our Lady of Medjugorji. Each time I was there when Mary appeared to Marija, it was an experience beyond description. I could feel the intense love that our Heavenly Mother has for each one of us. And even in a crowd of thousands, She made me feel like I was the only one kneeling on the grass in prayer and that my prayer mattered very much to Her.

In 2007 I made a trip back there to pray for special graces. It was worth the airline expense and car rental. On the last day during the apparition, I felt such peace that I prayed to Mary, "I don't want to go back home." It seems odd to say this, but that is exactly how I felt. I think it is because when our Blessed Mother comes, She brings the peace of Heaven with Her. We are given a foretaste of what awaits us beyond the edge of Earth. Suddenly in my heart I experienced these words from Her. "Go back and be a good grandmother." Little did I know that more grandchildren would come into my life and that now, my path to holiness is in simply being that good grandmother.

Chapter Nine

VISITATIONS

One day in August 2008 a young girl drowned in the Niagara River while on a camping hike with a group of children. Her name was Magdalena. There was a lot in the newspapers about this tragedy that was especially heartbreaking because she was an only child. Prayer vigils were held at the shoreline where she fell in and was swept away by the strong current. A massive search ensued in an effort to find her body.

A few nights later and on three successive nights I was awakened by the sound of a child weeping and saying, "Mama!" It finally occurred to me that perhaps this was Magdalena. I arranged for a Mass to be offered for the repose of her soul. Soon her body was found by a fisherman and identified. This experience made a lasting impression on me since having souls make noises in our previous homes was what I was accustomed to. To actually hear a soul's "voice" was quite unsettling to me.

Frequent and regular visitations from the Departed Souls started the night of All Souls Day, November 2, 2008. Shortly after falling asleep I heard loud moans and groans around my head. I thought at first that I was having a bad dream, but there were only noises and no images. Tossing and turning and punching my pillow in frustration, I would finally fall asleep. For the next two nights, the same thing happened. I was perplexed. Then one night shortly after I fell asleep, there was a very loud shout at the foot of my bed. I sat up like a jack knife, something I was amazed I could do as I have a back problem and must roll out of bed carefully. I switched on the light and jumped out of bed. I hurried to the kitchen where I keep a bottle of Holy Water. As I blessed the room and the bed, I proclaimed, "By the power of the Holy Name of Jesus, be gone from here!" Surely, I thought, I was being visited by demons. Since I was afraid to go back to bed, I went on the sun porch and looked through my traditional prayer book for any prayers that I could say for the Souls in Purgatory. I found one and prayed it fervently.

The next morning I told all of this to my husband. I knew that he would be receptive because of our experiences in Alabama. Since we were sleeping in separate bedrooms because of his snoring, I thought that I would go back to our bedroom to see if the noises were limited to the guest room for some reason.

That night, I was again bothered by noises around my head. I got up and prayed. After telling this to my husband the next morning, I decided to sleep back in the guest room using a small nightlight with the TV in there

36

turned on softly. I remembered being afraid of the dark, much like a child and here I was an adult. Needless to say, I got very little sleep for over a week as the noises continued. It was terrifying. I made a routine before retiring that consisted of blessing the room with Holy Water and putting on Our Lady's brown scapular to calm my nerves. I also knelt down by my bed and prayed some special prayers for the Souls in Purgatory. It then occurred to me to see if there was a pattern of some sort as to time, number and kinds of noises. I put a small pad of notepaper and a pen on the nightstand. From that day on, whenever I was disturbed, I would put on the light and record everything.

CHAPTER TEN

A SPIRITUAL DIRECTOR

After months on my own, I decided to pray to Father Nugent's departed soul in an effort to find another spiritual director. I remembered that once in confession at my parish, I did ask the confessor if he could recommend someone. He gave me the name of a Father DiGiulio. That was all he said. I did not find much encouragement from that because he did not offer any other information. Later on, I confided this to a friend. She said that she would ask a relative of hers who is a nun if she knew of anyone. It came back that Sister gave the name of Father DiGiulio who lived at St. Bernadette's Parish. There it was; a name that came up twice and where he could be contacted.

So I went online and pulled up information about that parish. There was a photo showing two priests standing side by side and smiling. I recognized one as Msgr.

Nugent. The name of the priest next to him was Father DiGiulio! I gasped in surprise and knew right then and there that dear Father Nugent had indeed led me to my new spiritual director. I immediately sent a letter to Father DiGiulio at St. Bernadette's including a copy of the email that Father Nugent had sent me confirming his belief in what I was experiencing with the Souls in Purgatory. Father DiGiulio called me within a few days saying that he would be happy to meet with my husband and me.

On April 28, 2010, we drove to Orchard Park, NY to meet with Father. He welcomed us warmly and escorted us to his office where he asked me to convey everything that had happened to me since November 2008. I did have my journal with me and that was very helpful. It was also an advantage to have Bob there as he confirmed what I was revealing to Father DiGiulio. I was as conscientious about telling my husband every morning about any nightly visitations as I was about recording them in my journal.

After I finished, the first thing that Father asked me was if our house was blessed and consecrated to the Sacred Heart of Jesus. I did tell him that the day we moved in, I placed a picture of the Sacred Heart of Jesus up on the fireplace mantel and now that same picture hangs in our kitchen. Then he said something that totally surprised me. "I want to come to your home and consecrate it to the Sacred Heart by saying a Mass there." A Mass! In our home? Of course, yes! That would be wonderful! Father wanted to arrange things to take place on June 11, the Feast of the Sacred Heart. He gave me contact information to send for the necessary prayers and a document for the consecration. Good thing God is so patient with us. With our busy schedules, this blessed event did not take place until August.

CHAPTER ELEVEN

THE CONSECRATION
August 24, 2010

The excitement of the honor of having a Mass said in our home is difficult to put into words. I wanted my children and their spouses and my grandchildren to be present. I also invited two very close friends. In appreciation for Father coming, I had dinner here for him with just Bob and me. I planned to serve dessert afterwards with the other guests.

When it was time for Mass, Father went into the guest room to vest. This is the bedroom where the visitations began in November 2008. When I took him in there, he said, "I feel a great sense of peace in here."

I had a table set up in front of our fireplace for the altar and covered it with my best white tablecloth. Two blessed candles were lit and all of us took our places. I noticed that my precious grandchildren were very attentive and reverent throughout all of this. At one point in this time of prayer, Father presented the information about the Consecration of the Family to the Sacred Heart. He then took Holy Water and proceeded to bless every room in the house. It was all so beautiful and moving.

After Mass, Father had our family of four sign the document of Consecration to the Sacred Heart. I have that in a beautiful frame now on the piano in our living room.

When I think of this great privilege of having a Mass said in our home I thank God over and over again. Never in the history of our family has this ever happened. Truly the choirs of angels hovered over us all as we shared in the liturgy on that summer evening.

CHAPTER TWELVE

OTHERS

Back in 2008 when all of this started with the Souls of the Departed, I was very troubled. I had absolutely no control over what was happening to me. I confided this to a dear friend of mine in Alabama. She suggested that I get the book by Nicholas Eltz entitled *Get Us Out of Here!* The subtitle of it reads *Maria Simma responds to this call from the Poor Souls in Purgatory.* This humble woman who lived in Austria actually saw the souls who came to her beginning in 1940 until 1953. I was very enlightened and consoled by her story. If anything, I realized that I was not alone in my encounters with the Souls of the Departed. More recently, I read a book entitled *Hungry Souls, Supernatural Visits, Messages, and Warnings from Purgatory* by Gerard J. M. Van Den Aardweg. Indeed, there have been many others to whom our Merciful God has allowed the Souls of the Departed to have contact with.

As time went by, I was surprised to learn that the woman who ultimately led me to my publisher had herself been chosen to assist the Souls of the Departed.

CHAPTER THIRTEEN

SILENT MESSAGES

I can remember people telling me about having dreams about deceased relatives. One of them was particularly interesting. A woman's sister died and appeared to her in a dream dressed in black. She prayed fervently for her soul. Later on, she had the same dream, but her sister appeared dressed in white. She told a priest about this and he interpreted it as meaning the first appearance meant that her sister was in Purgatory; the second one meant that she was in Heaven.

There was a woman that I knew who suffered very much with brain cancer. When she passed away, her family noticed the fragrance of roses around her bed. This is often referred to as the "odor of sanctity". According to ascetical theology, this is an indication that the soul is a saint having achieved a high degree of holiness because of their life.

Father DiGiulio asked me once if I have ever received confirmation from any souls that my prayer efforts have released them from Purgatory. I had to think hard about this as sometimes such messages can go unnoticed. One particular sign was quite apparent.

In a hallway to some bedrooms in our home we have hung portraits of Bob's family: his parents and two grandmothers as well as our children when they were little and family pictures of us through the years. The picture of his paternal grandmother always looked crooked to me every time I went by there. I had to keep straightening it. It wasn't until after Father asked me that question that it occurred to me that maybe grandmother Emilia was trying to get my attention. I told Bob about this and we agreed to have a Mass offered for her soul even though she had been dead for many years. Most certainly that is what she wanted because shortly afterwards and to this day that picture has never hung crooked again.

Some people report seeing a butterfly at the gravesite after a funeral, others see a cardinal. Then, again, there can be a dream with a message. I had a friend whom I thought I could trust. Later on I felt that she had betrayed me. When she passed away from cancer, I prayed for her soul but did not feel charitable enough towards her to have a Mass offered.

Then I had a dream where she approached me from behind and I could see her arms wrapped around me in a hug. I knew it was she because of the jewelry that she was wearing. I felt that she was seeking my forgiveness for what she had done to me. I asked her forgiveness as well and had a Mass offered for her soul.

I pray the Litany of Our Lady daily for the repose of the souls of my parents. I told Father DiGiulio that I wished I knew if they were in Heaven yet. He said, "Ask God to give you a sign." I am praying for this favor.

My sister Louise lost her son at age eighteen. She told me that after he died, she would find pennies around the house in unexpected places. She believes that he has also made his presence known to her in quite a novel way. She has an old gas stove down the basement that she uses when she cans tomatoes in the summer. It has a timer on it that buzzes after it has been set. Often when she is downstairs, the buzzer goes off. She believes that it is her son reminding her that he is around.

One of the most fascinating accounts of souls making us aware of their presence happened to my best friend Pat's family. Her Aunt Jane was very special to all of them. Because she never had children of her own, she would lavish affection and kindness on her nieces and nephews. She did have her favorites, however.

Pat's daughter Mary Beth was the first to get married. Not long before the wedding, Aunt Jane was diagnosed with terminal cancer, but she hung on as she was determined to see her niece get married. And she did. It was a wonderful gift to everyone when Aunt Jane showed up. It wasn't too long after the big day that Aunt Jane passed away.

The Catholic tradition is to distribute holy cards with the deceased person's name, birthday and day of death information on the back. Pat's family treasured the beautiful prayer cards that were mementoes of their beloved aunt. There were different pictures of Blessed Mother that were selected.

Pat's son Michael got married four years later. I knew that he was the apple of Aunt Jane's eye, the favored one. The day before the wedding after the dress rehearsal in church, a strange thing happened. Pat's husband noticed something on the floor in the main aisle. He went to pick it up and saw that it was a holy card. He turned it over and was amazed to see that it was one from Aunt Jane's funeral! How did it get there? None of the women brought their purses into the church that day. And this church was located in Indiana, whereas Aunt Jane was buried in Michigan.

Indeed, Aunt Jane wanted her Michael to know that she was there in spirit for his wedding day. And best of all, the picture on that card was of Our Lady of the Miraculous Medal, that feast day being November 27, Michael's birthday.

Chapter Fourteen

SACRIFICE, SUFFERING AND SANCTITY

I was always fascinated by stories of the saints. In my childhood, our parish church had numerous large statues of them. As kids we read little books entitled "Lives of the Saints." In all, my first impressions of them were lofty. I had it in my heart that I, too, wanted to become a saint. It was all so glorious. My mother had a small picture of St. Therese the Little Flower hanging on the wall in her bedroom. It showed Therese with her arms raised up holding a bouquet of roses and giving them to Our Lady. I loved that picture so much. To this day, I promote devotion to Therese by distributing holy cards of her.

My spiritual journey was enriched by my thirteen years in religious life. Being a nun was supposed to be what I hoped would make me a saint. In time, I learned that sanctity is in the struggle to be virtuous, whatever your state in life might be. I was happy to hear the words of Mother Angelica, the founder of EWTN (Eternal Word Television Network). "We are all called to be great saints. Don't miss the opportunity." And when Our Lady told me to go home and be a good grandmother, I finally realized that sanctification for me lies in first being a good wife, a good mother, a good grandmother and, yes, even a good friend.

The spirituality of St. Therese is known as the Little Way. She herself longed to be a missionary in order to go out and convert the world. But soon she noticed how much she could please God by simply doing very well and with great love what her state in life presented to her each day. Recently I read in "Mercy Minutes with Jesus" by Rev. George W. Kosicki, CSB that St. Faustina chose to be joyful when suffering. He states, "Our suffering, then, can be joyful and redemptive. It can have real value, especially for the salvation of souls. So, following the example of St. Paul, for St. Faustina and countless other saints, the real challenge becomes in deciding not to waste our sufferings. Here, it's not a question of taking on more sufferings. Rather it's offering the sufferings and the miseries to Jesus for the salvation of souls that we do, in fact, have to deal with each day."* This is good news for all of us. We need to get into the habit of recognizing and using whatever comes to us each day. I remember how the nuns used to tell us kids to "offer it up." Even my parents would say that when we'd fuss. So in regards to the Souls in Purgatory, I can accept without complaint

---

* *Mercy Minutes with Jesus* by Rev. George W. Kosicki, CSB, page 386

whatever I have to suffer and then offer that for the release of them.

In looking back on my entire life from childhood to this present day, I have had many sufferings. Yet these were not excruciatingly painful physical sufferings as some saints had. As a child I suffered from low self-esteem. I endured bullying from some kids on the playground and on the walk home from school. Playmates did not choose me for their teams. This was so hurtful.

One of the biggest sufferings of my life was being away from my family when God called me to be a nun. While other sisters enjoyed their family on visiting Sunday, I stayed in the chapel and wept because my parents were not always able to drive the distance. Even after leaving the convent, I was away from them because my husband's jobs always found us living in another state.

Today as old age creeps up on me, I find that my sufferings are becoming more physical in small ways. It is hard for me to get out of bed in the morning on most days. And I simply cannot do as much during the day as I used to when I was younger; that is very frustrating. I tire easily and have to rest in the afternoon. So the words "All for Jesus" have now become "All for the Souls in Purgatory." And I firmly believe that each and every act of patience, each and every stifling of a complaint about these aches and pains, each and every act of mortification is like a cold spray of water on the consuming fires of Purgatory.

CHAPTER FIFTEEN

INTERCESSORS OR FRIENDS IN HIGH PLACES

When I was a child, my siblings and I had a reverential fear of our dad. Many times when we wanted something, we would ask Mom to talk to him. Basically, she acted as our intercessor. Mothers do have a way with fathers when it comes to this sort of thing. It is interesting that we Catholics are often criticized for not going directly to God with our prayer requests. People of some other denominations are firm in their belief that if they want something, they go straight to God with no one in between. I find that this is curious, indeed, because I then ask them if in their congregation the pastor has ever invited everyone to pray for someone. Yes, of course, they tell me. Well, then, the congregation is acting as intercessors, plain and simple.

In our Catholic tradition we have our own mother who intercedes to the Father for us. It is the Blessed

Virgin Mary, Our Lady. It occurred to me that when God looked upon the world that needed redemption and then had decided to send His Only Son to save us, He could have just sent Jesus, full-grown and ready to be our Savior. Instead, the Father chose to have Jesus Christ born of a woman named Mary. And after His mission was accomplished on the cross, Jesus specifically gave Her to us as **our** mother. (John 19:26) There is a profound message here. God in His Almighty Wisdom knew that we all could relate better to a mother whenever we are stuck and in trouble. So having Our Lady as a Heavenly Intercessor is a great gift.

In addition, we have the saints who are available as intercessors during our journey in this Vale of Tears. In our modern times, we have even had living saints among us, Blessed Mother Teresa of Calcutta and Blessed Pope John Paul II for example. However, often-overlooked sources are the Souls in Purgatory. I would like to quote at length from a book entitled *Stories About Purgatory*. *

In praying for the dead . . . let us remember that every prayer we say, every sacrifice we make, every alms we give for the repose of the dear departed ones will all return upon ourselves in hundredfold blessings. They are God's friends, dear to His Sacred Heart, living in His grace and in constant communion with Him. And though they may not alleviate their own sufferings, their prayers in our behalf always avail. They can aid us most efficaciously. God will not turn a deaf ear to their

* Stories About Purgatory, Compiled from Traditional Sources by An Ursuline Nun of Sligo, Ireland

*intercession. Being Holy Souls, they are grateful souls.
The friends that aid them, they in turn will also aid. We
need not fear praying to them in all faith and confidence.
They will obtain for us the special favors we desire. They
will watch over us lovingly and tenderly; they will guard
our steps; they will warn us against evil; they will shield
us in moments of trial and danger and when our hour of
purgatorial suffering comes, they will use their influence
in our behalf to assuage our pains and shorten the period
of our separation from the Godhead.*

I struggled with the decision to publish my story.
It was because of Father DiGiulio's insistence that
this was what God wanted from me that I finally made
the decision to do so. On my manuscript he wrote the
following: "The souls in purgatory cannot mitigate their
time of purification. They depend upon us on earth to
pray for them to be released sooner."

CHAPTER SIXTEEN

LET'S MAKE A DEAL

Grandmother Rose had the right idea about making a deal with the Souls in Purgatory when she was in need. Someone told me that they read somewhere that a soul said, "You, the living, can do everything for us, as we can do everything for you. It is an exchange of prayer."

When my son and his wife decided to get married on the coast of Maine, they certainly were taking a chance that the weather would cooperate. I was determined that the day would be perfect for them, so I made a deal with the Faithful Departed much like my grandmother did. A year before the wedding date, I began some special nightly prayers for the Souls in Purgatory. Without fail, I prayed with deep faith in my heart that the weather would be perfect and that soon after the celebration, I would be going to the rectory to have a Mass offered for them in thanksgiving for the granted favor.

We all arrived in Maine a few days earlier to weather that was cool and rainy for September. Both the bride and the groom were anxious that the weather would spoil the romantic setting that they had planned for their nuptials. I believed otherwise, of course. I was testing the Grandmother Rose's theory.

The day of the wedding dawned bright and beautiful. As the guests gathered on the grassy knoll at the edge of the ocean cliff, I noticed something that stunned me. The sea was a mixture of azure blue with whitecaps that provided a breathtaking contrast. Every rocky boulder and even the lighthouse took on unearthly colors. I knew without a doubt that my Faithful Departed buddies had interceded. My convictions were reaffirmed when one of the guests who was a native of the state remarked to me that in all of his years in Maine, he had never seen such colors out on the ocean. It was surreal to say the least. I knew that upon our return home, I would definitely remember to fulfill my part of the deal.

I heard once that the greatest power on earth is prayer. How true that is especially when we consider the Souls in Purgatory as our intercessors.

CHAPTER SEVENTEEN

YEARNING, WAITING AND PRAYING

The dictionary defines yearning as "deep or anxious longing, desire". I can feel yearning for any number of things. When I was a child, I remember yearning for school to end so I could have a summer free from the classroom. Later as a teen, I yearned for the phone to ring with the hope that I would be asked to the prom. In later years, I yearned for blessings to come upon my husband and my children and grandchildren. When you yearn for something, your focus is on the relief of this yearning through answered prayers.

The Souls in Purgatory yearn for God, for that Eternity where they will see Him face to Face. They also yearn for us to remember them, not just on the anniversary of their passing into Eternal Life, but everyday. I understood this yearning of theirs in the many sounds that I experienced when they began visiting me in November of 2008. I found it difficult to convey to my spiritual director the essence of these sounds. Once when I was praying the "Hail Holy Queen" prayer to Our Lady, the line "To Thee do we send up our sighs, mourning and weeping in this valley of tears" struck me with particular insight. Yes, I thought. This is exactly how the Souls mourn and weep and yearn in Purgatory for our intercession on their behalf. If we can find it in our hearts to identify the many yearnings of our daily lives, then perhaps we can better understand the yearning of these Souls in Purgatory.

I have a friend who is a member of my writing group. She has a great gift as a freelance artist. Being a Catholic herself, I mentioned to her that I was writing a book about the Souls in Purgatory. Beth has to follow her inspirations whenever she is moved to draw. When she presented me with her picture, I knew that it had to be in my book. You can see and feel the yearning and the waiting of the Souls depicted in it. How can you not be moved to compassion and the promise to pray for the Souls in Purgatory?

Everyone can find their own way of praying for them. Having a Mass offered is the best way. My practice is to have a Mass offered for Forgotten Souls once a month. But I also say a prayer each time I pass a cemetery. The best one I know is the "St. Gertrude's Prayer." Our Lord Himself taught it to her saying that each time it is prayed, a thousand souls are released from Purgatory.

St. Gertrude's Prayer

Eternal Father, I offer You the most Precious Blood of Your Divine Son, Jesus, in union with the Masses said throughout the world today, for all the Holy Souls in Purgatory.

When I pray this prayer, I customize it by adding "especiallies", like especially for the victims of 911; my ancestors through all generations; victims of violence; military personnel, etc. When I read the obituary in the daily newspaper, I pray this prayer for the names there. It becomes a habit after awhile. Most often I pray for young people who have died unexpectedly.

CHAPTER EIGHTEEN

PUBLISHING

I was very reluctant to have my book published, mostly because I was afraid of how my two children would accept and understand what their mother had experienced. Father DiGiulio said that I must do so because there is a very important message here. Besides, it was Msgr. Nugent who reminded me that God had given me a "special blessing and apostolate."

Frankly, I was dragging my feet about getting this manuscript done. Where would I go with it? What publisher would even be interested? Someone suggested that I check out Catholic publishing companies. So I went online and researched the publishing guidelines of one I was familiar with. Immediately I was uncomfortable with the process. Right then and there I knew that I had to self-publish, but with whom?

A few days later, my dear friend Pat sent me something in the mail that indicated to me without a doubt that Our Lady would show me the way. It was a copy of *The Spirit of Medjurgorje* newsletter. In time, I decided to contact June Klins, the editor, because I read where she had a devotion to the Souls in Purgatory, specifically those who had committed suicide. After emailing her, we decided to talk on the phone. I had found a kindred spirit!

With confidence that Our Lady had pointed the way, I welcomed June's suggestion to go with the company she had used for the publishing of her three volumes of stories about Medjugorje from the 25 years of the newsletter. To learn more about June's apostolate for the Souls of the Departed, please check out her website "Divine Mercy for Lost Souls."

CHAPTER NINETEEN

SACRED SILENCE

I remember that when I was in training to become a religious, silence was very much a part of our day. Being only eighteen, I didn't appreciate the importance of this. Later in my life, I succumbed like everyone else to the constant noise and interruptions of our wired world. But in time, by God's grace, I was led to respect silence and to seek it out in simple ways. Our four-season porch is now my sacred space where I can go in and close the doors on my world for a short time. This is around three o'clock in the afternoon, which is known as the Hour of Mercy. I pray the Chaplet and then a rosary for the Souls in Purgatory.

To make Silence a part of your life and in your home, start by turning off the TV. I found this very hard to do because I used to have it on from early morning until I went to bed. I'm not a sitcom or soap opera fan, but I do like watching current events. The news of the world is of concern to me, but now once I know what is current, I don't allow the media to repeatedly bombard my soul with the lurid details anymore. Instead, I turn to prayer for the suffering world. When I am busy in my kitchen I listen to Gregorian chant music and other CD's that are classical and quiet. I have also learned that every task I perform especially as a housewife has merit. So I offer this up for the Souls.

I also limit the time I spend on the Internet. I did establish myself on Facebook, but soon realized that social networking took up too much of my time, time I'd rather spend reading spiritual books and enjoying silence.

I think of our Lord Jesus and how there were so many demands on Him when He walked the earth. Being Human as well as Divine, He needed His quiet moments and rest. In fact, He requested that His apostles always "have a boat ready" pretty much like an "escape mechanism" so that He could go off to pray and to refresh His spirit. (Mark 3:9). It is a struggle to set time aside for silence and prayer because we think that we could get more done if we didn't stop for the solitude. This is one of the biggest misconceptions of our modern times. Realistically, we will never get everything done because there is only so much time in a day. Therefore, we need to take time for our spiritual life. The rewards are worth the effort. Find a sacred space for yourself, climb into that "boat" and see what a big difference this will make in your life.

CHAPTER TWENTY

JOURNAL SELECTIONS

Author note: I have kept a journal since November of 2008. I hope that what you read here will give you a clear understanding of what I have experienced with the Souls of the Departed making themselves known to me so that I would pray for them and let the world know how much they need our prayers.

December 5, 2008—And so it is . . . that I have concluded, God has blessed me with the charism to be visited by Souls. Bob, Pat, Frances, Dawn, Louise and Mary Ann know of this and no one else. I have recorded the onset of the visitations in my Adoration Journal.

At first, I thought that all I needed was to pray more for them during the day and also a special prayer at bedtime to keep them from bothering me while I slept. Someone still came. Then I thought that once November passed, the visits would stop. Someone still came. Once I thought I'd just ignore the first moan and maybe the soul would go away. The moan was heard twice and louder. Now, at the slightest faint sound, I acknowledge the Soul, and I pray, fervently.

December 16, 2008—I was awakened this morning at 5:19 a.m. by a sort of hum/moan near my ear—by now to me a very familiar thing. Perhaps it is that this soul has just passed into Eternity and learns how available I am for supplication. I had a thought: Will God allow me to live a very long life, like Mom into her 90's, so that I can pray many, many souls into Heaven?

December 22, 2008—5:30 a.m. "Arise!" It seems to be the plea. "Arise and sacrifice the comfort and warmth of your bed and pray for us." Yes. The "voice" today was feminine, almost like the sound of a mosquito buzz. In prayer, I thought that perhaps it might be Adeline, Joan's mom who passed away a few days ago. As much as I desire to know who these Souls are, I am content, knowing that someday in Eternity, I shall recognize them all! What a joyful occasion it will be!

December 29, 2008—I'm reflecting today on how this encounter with the Souls has transpired since early November. In the beginning it was so very loud and intrusive. I was so unsettled by this and even annoyed. But then over time, a warm and peaceful friendship evolved, and I was no longer anxious about going to sleep in the dark. Often, when I was especially tired, I'd ask them to please not disturb me during the night. I have been keeping a log of the times and kinds of visits. Some nights there are none; other times one or more.

As of today, I've learned that I must get up before 6:00 a.m. to make a special 6:00-7:00 Holy Hour of Prayer before the 7:00 a.m. Hour of Angels. I guess because once I start my day and get so busy, these prayers are often not said. The Souls have been most demanding. Can't blame them.

January 18, 2009—5:58 a.m.—It has been quiet, although now and then a female whisper during the night. But this morning, quite a very loud male plea/cry, so pathetic that I immediately arose to do a Holy Hour. So pathetic!

January 24-25, 2009—I hadn't had any visitors for a few nights, except one female voice that whispered, "I don't know how!"

January 26-27, 2009—Twice this night, a male moan came, strong in petition. I felt that it was a plea for the Chaplet of the Divine Mercy.

February 1, 2009—4:12 a.m.—A soul awoke me and I was perturbed! "Enough!" I thought to it. "I pray for you daily. If you disturb my sleep, I will not pray for you!" Then I proceeded to pray the Chaplet of the Divine Mercy for all Souls. However, when I did doze off while praying it, a Soul gently nudged me to awaken.

February 2, 2009—Last night from 5:45 a.m. it was busy it seems, but gently so. As much as I desire to enjoy uninterrupted rest, they come . . .

Forgotten

It has occurred to me to discuss with my spiritual director my deep desire to know God's will in all of this. Since I was 18 years old, I remember that God's Will was very important in my life. Is God leading me to something more? Does He desire an apostolate of sorts?

February 17-18, 2009—Last night shortly after retiring and in the midst of having fallen asleep while praying the Chaplet, I heard a groan, quite loud. So I finished the Chaplet for that soul. Thereafter, I was awakened by it three times with very little time in between. I was annoyed! I finally sprinkled with Holy Water and whispered, "What more do you expect me to do right now? I need to sleep."

This morning around 6:45 the same soul, familiar groan, quite loudly awakened me. Poor thing! So, so sad.

March 6, 2009—We returned last night from our two weeks away in Florida. Yes, I had visitations wherever we went, especially at Pat's home in Jacksonville. Last night there was one male moan shortly after I fell asleep. This morning around 4:30, a very sad, female moan. Just so pathetic.

March 29, 2009—Visits have been off and on, same soul it seems. He is not satisfied with the St. Gertrude's Prayer. They all want the Chaplet of the Divine Mercy. And if I doze off, the soul "sounds off" to alert me to finish it.

March 30, 2009—Strangely, last night it was a hum. I prayed the Chaplet, so many times.

April 2, 2009—It would have been three nights with no visits until around 6:03 a.m. today. I had just fallen asleep after being awake from 3:15, watching EWTN, etc. to get sleepy once again. Suddenly, I was awakened by a groan, less mournful than the others and I immediately began the Chaplet of the Divine Mercy. Being exhausted, I know I had dozed off in this prayer. What I heard next was new to these experiences, the soul, a female, tried to use words, but they were difficult to understand given the speed with which they were said. I prayed, dozed off and then heard another sound, almost humorous like "Uh oh! No you don't! Keep praying!" May she rest in peace!

April 8, 2009—"Mary", the voice used a name! At first it was the usual sound, like a muffled groan that alerted me to pray the Chaplet. I dozed, of course, then was awakened once again to finish the prayer. Suddenly and softly a female voice followed by "Mary". I wondered, "Mary who?" Then it came to me! My friend Mary perhaps who recently passed away. And I prayed Hail Mary's for her soul.

May 19, 2009—Something very new early this morning around 6:00 a.m. A young female voice said, "Hey, Del." I was startled that this soul could say my name! I prayed the Chaplet for her, dozed off and was awakened by her to finish it. Oh, how these souls love that Chaplet of the Divine Mercy!

June 15, 2009—It has been a month since I've recorded anything. However, I still get visitations, although not as frequently in succession. But this morning around 5:45 a.m. some souls were determined to get me out of bed.

After a few of the usual grunts, moans and groans near my head, I perceived a "Let's rock 'n' roll!" Too funny! I love their sense of humor! Of course, by then I knew that I'd have to kick off those covers and get up to make a serious 6:00-7:00 Holy Hour.

June 30, 2009—Yes, my visitations continue. This week it seems like the same, persistent soul. I can tell because the nature and tone of the sound is the same. This morning it was around 5:40 a.m., quite loud and badgering to me. I said aloud, "Oh, my. I do love you and here is a Chaplet of the Divine Mercy for you." So I prayed. Yesterday, I attended a Mass at St. Augustine that I had offered for Forgotten Souls. I had tears in my eyes when Father Dan mentioned the Mass intention. How sad to be forgotten by anyone for any reason. I shall always try to remember them each day, each pain, each mortification, each aggravation.

July 12, 2009—This morning a gentle, female voice, so rare, as most souls are male. Very loud and long in my right ear. Some souls badger, I think, because they are so desperate. Jesus, I accept this gift—special friend of the Departed Souls.

September 25, 2009—Lately a Soul has used the gentle touch activated light in our dining room hutch to get our attention. To turn it on, you need to softly touch the door hinge on the right. It has three settings: low, medium and high. Last night I got up around 1:30 a.m. for some toast and milk. There it was! The dim hutch light was on! Out loud I said, "And who are you who turned this on?" I turned it off and went back to bed. Just as I was dozing off, a very soft and meek female voice cried a sob. So pathetic, always so pathetic! I said, "I love you. Here is a Chaplet of the Divine Mercy just for you." Mother Mary of Mercy, how humbling it is to know that You send these souls to me!

October 9, 2009—Here's a new one. I was sitting in my rocker watching a ballgame with Bob and dozing off and on. I must've fallen asleep (It was near 11:00 p.m.) when quite suddenly I was awakened by a puff of cold air right in my face! Immediately I felt a presence, quite friendly, of course, and so I prayed the St. Gertrude's Prayer for this Departed Soul who used a novel way to get my attention. When I opened my eyes upon feeling this icy air, I looked up to see if, perhaps, the ceiling fan was on. It was not. Then I looked to see if Bob was in the room; he was not. My goodness! Is this not the most curious encounter?

November 2, 2009—All Souls Day—Surprisingly, today was uneventful. I had expected a "convention of souls" during the night, but there were none. Well, I believe that Our Lady will continue sending them along, even now and then, as She pleases. All are welcome!

January 11, 2010—Early this morning I heard a soul near the bedroom window. I smiled as I thought of how meek it was, while others seem to be so "in my face."

February 24, 2010—Jacksonville, FL—I had a couple of brief visits at Pat and Len's while on vacation with Bob. And here at Orange Lake Resort, there was a reprieve of sorts. But I had a sleepless night, so I got up to read around 5:30 a.m. I went back to bed and fell asleep and dreamt some. I know that I was disturbed a few times by the same soul, but what was unique was a quite audible and pleading cry of a child, a girl, "Mama!" It brought tears to my eyes.

March 13, 2010—Sometimes these souls are so persistent! I didn't sleep well at night and finally got dozy around 5:00 a.m. But wouldn't you know it; I heard a few gentle sounds to get up and pray. I ignored them, as I was SO tired. Suddenly, very loudly, a fluttering sound as thru lips. Souls do have a way with me and a sense of humor! It was 6:01 a.m.

March 23, 2010—This morning, someone new, it seems. Amazing how different each "voice" is. I welcome them all.

April 16, 2010—Oh, my goodness! What a startle! I had just nestled into bed and began the Chaplet deciding that doing this would help any soul present from disturbing me. I dozed off and, "BUZZ!" once and loud right into my left ear. That kept me awake until I finished the prayer. Oh, my dear Poor Souls!

May 8, 2010—Should have turned on the light and written the words down because now I'm not sure. A woman, very audible, twice, "I can't tell you." Puzzling. Can't tell me what? But not sure except for the "I can't" part.

May 23, 2010—I'm currently on a steroid for inflammation of my herniated disc. The pill for nighttime puts me in a very deep sleep. Since my Souls seem to come at the "twilight" time, that is, at the point between sleep and being awake, there is no twilight when on this medication. Last night a long and most pleading moan that I could hear from afar and then it got louder and louder as I was pulled from the effects of the medication. I apologized to that dear Soul who had to be so persistent. It brings me to this thought of who gets to come to me. I was told that Our Lady does this. I can just imagine Her going to Purgatory and inviting particular souls to visit me. That seems so special, and, I again, am humbled.

May 31, 2010—I awoke around 2:30 a.m. having heard a couple visitors. Upon going to the kitchen for a drink, I noticed that the dining room hutch light was on! After going back to bed and just before falling asleep, one very long and painful moan. The pity of it all tears at my heart, and I feel such a responsibility to pray!

June 21, 2010—around 5:00 a.m. a guest. Shortly after retiring that night, one soul came just as I was about to fall asleep. Sometimes they come then or when I'm fully awake. Sometimes I can feel a presence before I hear someone.

June 24, 2010—Most unusual! Heard a sound from the left side of the room like a stick being rubbed along a wooden fence! What a unique way to get my attention.

July 8, 2010—The room seemed to have been filled with many souls pleading at once!

July 12, 2010—3:45 a.m. I was awakened by a rather loud moan, so I began the Chaplet. I fell asleep soon afterwards, and then the same moan, more persistent. I awoke and continued the Chaplet, but soon dozed off again. Suddenly I was awakened by the loudest, longest and pathetic moan! I was not at all frightened like I had first been that night in November 2008. Instead I felt a deep sense of sorrow that this soul so yearned for my prayer and I was too tired to pray for it.

July 14, 2010—I've learned how these souls have their own personalities. The other night the one was so persistent until I had finished the Chaplet. This morning a soul awoke me. I said, "I love you,' and then I began the Chaplet. I fell asleep and it must've stayed nearby, waiting patiently for me to awaken and to realize that I had only done one decade. I finished it for those dear Souls who must put up with my weaknesses

July 17, 2010—Last night I had a soul come and awaken me to pray the Chaplet. I know I fell asleep, yet it did not pester me. Later on, I woke up and finished that prayer. What a wonderful reunion someday in Heaven to actually meet the souls I have prayed for!

August 5, 2010—There was just the sweetest melody! Was it an angel?

August 7, 2010—Last night the two visitations were melodiously sung. Could it be that these were happy souls, freed from Purgatory by my prayers?

August 11, 2010—4:08 a.m. I heard a very young female voice, a cry. I prayed and thought of the 21-year-old woman killed with two men in a car accident last weekend or maybe it was one of the women missionaries killed by the Taliban last week in Afghanistan . . . .

August 13, 2010—This is the second time this week that I heard a joyful sound. Hard to describe, but it occurred to me—this surely is a Soul that has been released from Purgatory. Thank You, Jesus.

August 23, 2010—Many souls came this night. Could it be that they know the Mass is being said? Sometimes I grow weary, but I accept this great grace with the Love of Jesus.

August 28, 2010—It has been quiet since the Mass here in our home and the consecration to the Sacred Heart. However, I think two souls visited since, but I can't be certain. Last night I experienced a young voice, a girl. Most unusual. There was an obituary in yesterday's paper of an eleven-year-old girl who passed away.

September 9, 2010—I went to bed after midnight as I was waiting for Bob to come home after picking David up at the airport. Of course, I prayed my usual ahead-of-your-visit-to-me-dear-soul Chaplet. I was just about to doze off when there came a mournful groan, same one as the night before. So, another Chaplet. I offered up my annoyance to Jesus.

February 18, 2011—This morning around 5:00 a.m. I was surprised to hear near the left side of my head a familiar low hum. I was delighted. Then about 15 minutes later, overhead, there was a high-pitched sound. I prayed only briefly, as I had had a bad night for sleeping. Thank You, Jesus and Mary.

March 17, 2011—I awoke around 6:00 a.m. and went into the kitchen. The dining room chandelier was on. The room had an eerie glow because the dimmer switch was moved to its lowest setting. "Ok, dear Soul, whoever you are, I shall pray for you." And I switched off the light with a smile.

August 10, 2011—I was about to drift off to sleep, when I heard a loud hum into my ear. It sounded like a male voice. I immediately thought of the thirty warriors shot down in that helicopter in Afghanistan . . . .

October 7, 2011—I have a bad cold and laid down for a nap. I was still awake when I clearly heard a voice, a young person, trying to say "Please help!" or "Help, please! I prayed the Chaplet.

January 18, 2012—Had a restless night. The wind kept me awake. Dozed off and on. Suddenly, close to my left ear, a moan, about three seconds long. "Dear Soul, I love you!" I prayed the Chaplet fervently.

February 7, 2012—I was very tired, so I took a nap. Awoke at 2:45 and remembered that I needed to pray the Chaplet at 3:00. I dozed off. At 2:57 I heard a soft, high squeal sound. Prayed the Chaplet.

February 13, 2012—Two very different voices and tones. Female.

February 17, 2012—A lone Soul came. Sounded like one of the two from February 13 . . .

March 24, 2012—Something entirely new! A female voice sounding JOYFUL! Thank You, Jesus!

April 15, 2012—I had a sleepless night, tossing and turning. As I felt myself slipping into sleep, I thought I heard a Soul, but I chose to ignore it. Bad idea! Suddenly I heard a high-pitched buzzing cry, as if really in agony! "I'm so sorry! I love you! Here is a Chaplet." Thank You, Mother of Mercy.

June 13-14, 2012—A persistent Soul for whom my praying the Chaplet more than once did not seem to help. "I'll get a Mass for you." I sent a note and a Mass stipend off to Father D. this morning.

July 8, 2012—Two males.

July 19, 2012—I was awakened around 6:50 a.m. by a distant, persistent humming. I immediately began a Chaplet after apologizing for taking so long to wake up. I'm a little groggy this morning . . .

August 9, 2012—I had a hard time falling asleep this night. Around 6:36 a.m. I was awakened from a deep sleep by a distant-sounding moan that was constant with no pauses for a breath. I struggled to wake up. "I love you," I said and quickly prayed the Chaplet.

October 18-19, 2012—Went to bed after 10:00. Hadn't nodded off when I hard a heavy male voice, strong in tone. I prayed. Late in the night I was awakened by a female voice. I began the Chaplet, but then fell asleep, only to be awakened again. This happened with that poor soul having to awaken me again and again. So today, I shall offer my whole day for those two visitors, especially for that woman who had to keep after me so much.

October 27, 2012—Many souls; many Chaplets. Their cries touch my heart so much!

November 2, 2012—All Souls Day. No one.

November 22, 2012—A soul in the corner, near the dresser. I think it was a woman.

December 14, 2012—A very busy night that I lost count!

I continue to record all visitations in my journal . . .

CHAPTER TWENTY-ONE

THE CHAPLET OF THE DIVINE MERCY

As you have read in the selections from my journal, I pray the Chaplet of the Divine Mercy for the Souls of the Departed. I have learned that this is what they desire most as a prayer to begin with. Beyond this, I have had Holy Masses offered for them to gain their release from Purgatory. The story of Jesus and His Divine Mercy for the world is recorded in a book entitled *Saint Maria Faustina Kowalska, Diary, Divine Mercy in My Soul* published by the Marians of the Immaculate Conception in Stockbridge, MA.

St. Faustina, Helen Kowalska, was born in the village of Glogowiec, Turek County, Lodz Province, Poland on August 15, 1905. She became a nun in the Congregation of the Sisters of Our Lady of Mercy in Warsaw, Poland. In the 1930's she began to have visions of Jesus during which He taught her how much love and mercy He had for the whole world. He instructed her to write down everything that He said to her. Jesus called her His little secretary.

In time, He taught her how to pray the Chaplet of the Divine Mercy on a regular rosary. He told her that the hour of His greatest mercy is at three o'clock in the afternoon, the time when He died on the cross.

First pray one Our Father, then one Hail Mary followed by the Apostles Creed. Then on the Our Father beads say: **"Eternal Father, I offer You the Body and Blood, Soul and Divinity of Your dearly beloved Son, Our Lord Jesus Christ, in atonement for our sins and those of the whole world."** On the Hail Mary beads say: **"For the sake of His sorrowful Passion have mercy on us and on the whole world."**

In conclusion say three times: **"Holy God, Holy Mighty One, Holy Immortal One, have mercy on us and on the whole world."**

Jesus also told her to pray this Chaplet for the sick and the dying as well as for the Souls in Purgatory.

EPILOGUE

So that's my story. As earthly inhabitants we are all destined someday to cross over to the other side into Eternity. Consider making friends with those who have gone before us and who are in need of our prayers right now. I read once that when we are dying, we are like a ship that is fading from view on the horizon. Those who see that vessel departing proclaim, "There she goes!" Well, I expect that people who gather around my bedside when my time comes will say the same about me. Yes, there she goes. However, I am very comforted by the fact that the Souls of the Departed whom I have helped with my prayers and with the writing of this book will be watching and waiting for me on the Horizon of Eternity saying, "Look! Here she comes!" And what a grand homecoming that will be!

AFTERTHOUGHT

After my manuscript was submitted to the publisher and I was in the process of working with the design consultant, two very significant things happened that I believe I must include in this book. On Sunday, March 3, 2013 I had a visitation that was very special to me. Around 5:15 a.m. I heard from the left side of my room a woman's voice that said, "Ami," and then again "Ami." Her voice was young, gentle and sweet. At first I was puzzled by the words, and then it occurred to me that "Ami" is French for "friend". Yes, this precious soul was confirming that I am a friend of the Souls in Purgatory.

(My mother suffered from dementia before she passed away, and she didn't know who I was anymore. The last time we visited her, I was surprised when she looked at me and said, "I love you, Del," as her nurse tucked her into bed one night. Those were her last words to me. In 2004 we traveled from Birmingham, Alabama for

Thanksgiving to be with my family. Mom was failing quickly. I sat at her bedside and prayed the Chaplet of the Divine Mercy over and over again for her. I knew that Jesus said to St. Faustina, **"Pray as much as you can for the dying. By your entreaties obtain for them trust in My mercy, because they have most need of trust, and have it the least. Be assured that the grace of eternal salvation for certain souls in their final moment depends on your prayer."** (*Diary*, **1777**). Mom passed away early Saturday morning.)

The second event happened on Thursday, March 7, 2013 on my way to holy Mass in the morning. As always, I prayed along the route for the Departed Souls of my family and my friends, my parents always being first. Somehow I felt that Dad was in Heaven, but I wasn't certain about Mom. Right out loud I said, "Mom, I wish I knew if you were in Heaven." As you recall reading earlier in this book, I expressed to Father DiGiulio my desire to know if my parents were in Heaven and he told me to ask God for a sign. Now and then during prayer I would ask God for this favor, but I never pressed the issue, being content that if and when God wanted to, He would reveal this to me.

It was my turn to be the lector that week. After Mass a gentleman came up to me, someone I had seen frequently at morning Eucharist but had never spoken to nor did I know his name.

"Has your mother passed away?" he asked.

"Yes, she lived to be ninety-two," I answered, puzzled by his question.

"Well, she was standing behind you when you were reading today."

I was shocked and surprised at his words. He then revealed to me that he has the gift of healing and that he also sometimes sees rays of light coming from the Host and the Chalice at the Consecration of the Mass.

"So is my mother in Heaven?"

"Oh, of course!" he answered. "She stood by you and then floated up above the sanctuary in a bright light and disappeared." Unlike how I felt Dad's presence when I stood on that ladder many years ago while painting, I did not feel my mother's presence as I stood and read the scripture. Of course, that was a good thing, because being distracted at that time would have interfered with my proclaiming the Word of Lord. When I got back home, I told this to my husband. He held me in his arms as I cried tears of joy. Indeed, on that morning in that very holy place, God let my mom assure me with the help of a holy man that she was in Heaven. Praise and glory be to God forever! Amen.

POETRY

EVERY PRAYER MATTERS

When you are moved to say a prayer—
Pray it.
For throughout your day you see
And you hear of people and needs
That require a prayer or two.
In our busy and worldly world
So full of distractions
We should "Come to the water"
Deep within the silence of our soul
Where whispering that one, brief prayer
Matters to someone, somewhere, right now.

God hears that prayer
And He requires that of you.
So pray it.
Because those many simple prayers
When added to the cacophony of
The Universe
Join in the eternal "Sanctus! Sanctus!"
Of the angelic choirs.

Your prayer matters.
Please, pray it.

JESUS IN MY KITCHEN

I enter its solitude, Lord—
The counters and cupboards
Stove, fridge and sink.
It is here I can praise You
With the work of my hands.
You have given me a love for cooking
And creating meals to pleasure the body
And soothe the soul.

I adore You in the vegetables and fruits
And I especially am reminded of Your
Great love for all of humanity when I bake bread—
You, our Bread of Life.
The cakes and other pastries that give me
More pleasure than ever remind me of the
Delights of Heaven
Sweetness beyond all imagination!

I want to be a saint, Lord.
Sanctify my days spent here in my kitchen.
Let its order and cleanliness
Be a sign of my deep love for You.
Let the meals I prepare with such joy
Be a reflection of the praise
I have in my heart, Eternal God.
Sanctus!
Sanctus!
Sanctus!

RESOURCES

Websites

www.divinemercyforlostsouls.com
www.friendsofthesufferingsouls.com
www.thepurgatoryproject.com
www.prayforsouls.org www.medjugorje.org
www.marian.org

Books

<u>Catechism of the Catholic Church.</u> New Jersey: Paulist Press, 1949.

Eltz, Nicky <u>Get Us Out of Here.</u> Illinois: The Medjugorje Web, 2005.

Groeschel C.F.R., Father Benedict J. <u>After This Life.</u> Indiana: Our Sunday Visitor, 2009.

Hughes, Serge <u>Catherine of Genoa, Purgation and Purgatory.</u> New Jersey: Paulist Press, 1979.

Kosicki, CSB, Rev. George W. <u>Mercy Minutes with Jesus</u>. Massachusetts: Marian Press, 2008.

Kowalska, Saint Maria Faustine, <u>Diary Divine Mercy in My Soul.</u> Massachusetts: Marians of the Immaculate Conception, 2002.

Schouppe, S.J. Father F.X. <u>Purgatory Explained by the Lives and Legends of the Saints.</u> North Carolina: TAN Books, 1986.

Ursuline Nun of Sligo, Ireland <u>Stories About Purgatory.</u> North Carolina: TAN Books, 2009.

Van Den Aardweg, Gerard J.M., <u>Hungry Souls.</u> North Carolina: TAN Books, 2009.

CPSIA information can be obtained at www.ICGtesting.com
Printed in the USA
LVOW082224020413

327318LV00001B/161/P